The Lady Smith

Award-winning playwright and actor Andrew Moodie has written a number of plays, including *Riot, Oui, Wilbur County Blues,* and *A Common Man's Guide To Loving Women.* He lives and works in Toronto.

The Lady Smith

~

Andrew Moodie

BLIZZARD PUBLISHING
Winnipeg • Niagara Falls

First published 2000 in Canada and 2001 in the United States by
Blizzard Publishing Inc.
73 Furby Street, Winnipeg, Canada R3C 2A2.

Distributed in the United States by General Distribution Services,
4500 Witmer Industrial Estates, Niagara Falls, NY 14305–1386.

Cover art: detail from "Rise, shine for thy light has come" (c. 1930) by Aaron Douglas by permission of The Gallery of Art, Howard University, Washington, D.C. Cover design by Otium.

Printed for Blizzard Publishing in Canada.

5 4 3 2 1

Blizzard Publishing gratefully acknowledges the support of the Manitoba Arts Council, the Canada Council for the Arts, and the Government of Canada through the Book Publishing Industry Development Program for our publishing program.

Cataloguing in Publication Data

Moodie, Andrew.
The lady smith.
A play.
ISBN 1-55331-002-0
I. Title.

PS8576.O558L33 2000 C812'.54 C00–920172–6
PR9199.3.M613L33 2000

to Marjorie Moodie,
my mother

The Lady Smith was first produced by Theatre Passe Muraille, from March 21 to April 16, 2000, with the following cast:

CYNTHIA	Carol Anderson
SYLVIA	Janet Bailey
JORDAN	David Collins
HOLLY	Karen Glave

Directed by Layne Coleman
Set design by David Broechler
Lighting design by Peter Freund
Costume design by maxine bailey
Sound design by Steven GordonMarsh

Player's Manifesto Part III

Precision, relaxation, truth.

Precision of thought.
Precision of action.

An atmosphere of trust that allows a performer to enter a state of calm that unlocks their darkest, deepest, most intuitive, most sacred self.

Whatever truth may exist, however it may exist, even if the only truth is that there is no truth, shall make itself known. Accept it, embody it, communicate it.

Characters

SYLVIA: a middle-aged black woman

HOLLY: a mid-twenties black woman

CINDY: a mid-twenties black woman

JORDAN: a middle-aged black man

Voices on the answering machine:
MARY
MRS. SHORT
ARLENE
JEAN-MARC
LANDLORD

Setting

The play takes place in Toronto around Bathurst and Bloor.

The apartment is cluttered with Holly's art and Cindy's photo equipment. There is an exit to the kitchen, to Cindy's darkroom, to the front door, to the balcony, and there is a staircase leading to a balcony and rooms upstairs. There should be a couch and an area for Holly's computer.

Playwright's Notes

What I intend is that the painting Holly shows us at the beginning of the play is a slide projection. A black woman singing a very sorrowful song. The painting can be done in any style, it should look like an oil painting, and it must give the impression of great, great sorrow.

Throughout the play I have indicated in the stage directions that the projection of the painting changes to something else: an image of a window, a computer, etc. The images should cross-fade into each other in a dreamlike manner. If you have the ability to do so, it would be wonderful to have the images projected onto a few of Holly's paintings on stage, so that all of her artwork can, at times, morph into other images that complement the scene, but I realize that this can be expensive.

After Sylvia asks Holly, "How did you two meet?" on page 30, characters start to appear and disappear in a very dreamlike fashion. There are many different ways of dealing with this; you can leave characters on stage, you can sneak characters off stage, it's up to you. The one thing I ask is that it be done very smoothly. What is intended is that they be dreamlike flashbacks and that they reveal to Sylvia the nature of Jordan's relationship with Holly.

There are times when the dialogue is not as important as the character's action. When Sylvia is putting a virus on the computer, and talking on the phone with her daughter, what is important is setting up the tension that Holly might catch her. The phone conversations should add to the tension, not take away from it.

The song Sylvia sings on page 41 is Mamie Smith's "Crazy Blues." At the end, when Cindy puts Sylvia's CD into the player, it should be Sylvia singing the full version of the song with musical accompaniment. I understand however that this may also be expensive and should only be done if a good quality recording can be made. If not, use whatever you feel will best suit the scene.

Holly is a very talented artist. Her paintings should be very good ones. Her attitude towards her own work is very harsh, but only because of years of rejection.

Here are some notes on the characters in the play. They may be obvious to you, but I wanted to put them down anyway, so at the very least my intentions are clear.

SYLVIA: You enter the play after having just seen your husband with another woman. Allow yourself to still be soaking all this new information in. Your reality has just been shattered. If you play too calm and cool off the top, then you don't allow Holly to feel a kind of eerie focus from you that she will need for her next scene. I gave your character a lot of halting dialogue for a reason. I know how annoying it can be halfway through a two-month run to never complete a sentence that the character desperately wants to complete, but it is essential. The question she wants to ask at the top of the play is: "Are one of you fucking my husband?" She stops herself for a reason. The first scene with Jordan is a flashback; enjoy his love.

HOLLY: You start the play explaining to a total stranger your feelings of inadequacy doing the one thing you love more than anything in the world. You love your art, you feel you're a failure; that is your struggle. I see Holly as an eggshell, apply force on the ends it's strong as a rock, apply force on the sides and it shatters. You are lost in your own world. You actually are very talented. You don't know who Sylvia is until the very end.

CINDY: At the start of the play you are at the end of your relationship with Holly. You are sick of being the mature adult figure in her life. Your contempt is important. Let Holly be childish and fly off the handle and try and keep a restrained tone. Sylvia is your oasis of sanity. The more you allow Holly's wild dementia to unnerve you, the more you need Sylvia's companionship.

JORDAN: There is more going on than just wanting to have sex with a young attractive woman. He's making a break for the field beyond the prison wall. He has doubts, about whether what he's doing is right. There are times when Jordan becomes angry. The actor should just keep an eye on how deep the rage becomes. It should never look like he could be violent towards Sylvia, but don't pull back on the rage either. It's a fine line. Just keep an eye on it. That's all.

And finally, have fun. Go after each other. Play with each other. the show depends on it.

—Andrew Moodie,
October 2000

Act One

(At rise: music. SYLVIA enters.)

SYLVIA:
Most people
When they sing
Try to create power and volume from their throats.
They lift themselves up onto their toes
Fling their arms to their sides
And try to leave the ground
But to sing the blues
To sing the blues
You take a deep breath
You got to plant your feet
You got to dig down deep
You got to plunge yourself into that
Special well of pain
The way a child
Will wallow
In dust, mud, and grime
Unafraid of
Consequences
Eager to learn, to understand its true nature
Eager to become one with the thing itself

(HOLLY and CINDY enter. CINDY has her camera in hand. She is cleaning it.)

HOLLY: But I haven't made an oil painting in what … seven months.

CINDY: And she's not going to.

HOLLY: I don't plan on it.

CINDY: The fumes were …

HOLLY: It's the turpentine. It's pretty bad.

CINDY: But you haven't worked in oils for a while.

HOLLY: This is the last one actually. By the time I finished it, my feeble attempts to embrace conceptualism kind of died away from within me, so …

SYLVIA: I see.

HOLLY: When there is a wave of change in the art of a culture, it reminds artists like myself that you are not an innovator but a soulless imitator, striving to be recognized for the cheap mimicry of standards laid out by others and your own inadequacy. But I still kinda like it, I guess.

(Silence.)

CINDY: It's Sylvia, right?

SYLVIA: Yes.

CINDY: Sylvia …

SYLVIA: … Smith.

CINDY: So what exactly does someone in human resources do, Sylvia?

SYLVIA: I'm actually an office manager. Human resources is a part of my job as office manager.

(Silence.)

CINDY: So let's see, uh, heat and hydro's not included. We just split it three ways. We try not to use the dryer, as you saw we have one of those big wooden rack things that we usually set up in the bathroom.

SYLVIA: All right.

CINDY: We're kinda looking for someone to move in right away. You'd still have to pay last month's rent but first month we'd reduce to say three hundred bucks.

SYLVIA: All right.

CINDY: Is there anything else you need to see? Anything else you want to know?

SYLVIA: Not really.

CINDY: You sure?

(The phone rings.)

SYLVIA: Do you …

(HOLLY goes to get the phone. Realizes who it is. Stops.)

CINDY: Yes?

SYLVIA: I'll …

CINDY: No it's okay, the machine'll … go ahead.

(HOLLY runs over to the answering machine to turn down the sound. The answering machine starts.)

SYLVIA: Are either one of you …

(She chooses not to ask the question she was going to ask.)

Do you smoke?

CINDY: Smoke?

SYLVIA: Yes.

CINDY: Cigarettes?

HOLLY: I do.

CINDY: Holly does. And we aren't big on pot in the apartment. If you have to spark one up, try to use the back porch area, that's the smoking room. Toss the roaches in the tin can.

SYLVIA: No, it's uh …

CINDY: It's no problem, really. Just use the back porch.

HOLLY: Oh, and there are a couple of guys next door. Pete and that other guy, what's-his-face. If they smell you sparking up, they'll come over. They're harmless but persistent.

SYLVIA: I don't smoke pot.

CINDY: Okay.

SYLVIA: I don't.

CINDY: That's okay too. Just, if you want to, you can.

(Silence.)

HOLLY: Well, thanks for coming. We'll let you know when we've made our decision.

SYLVIA: I'll take it.

CINDY: Uhm.

SYLVIA: I would like to … I'll take the room.

CINDY: Okay.

HOLLY: Well, we have to talk about it and …

CINDY: No no, that's okay. Do you have first and last?

SYLVIA: I could write you a cheque.

(She takes out her cheque-book.)

CINDY: Fine.

(SYLVIA realizes this is not a good idea.)

SYLVIA: Actually, I don't think I have any cheques left. Could I give you cash?

CINDY: That would be great actually.

(The phone rings. HOLLY picks it up and hangs it up immediately. Smiles.)

SYLVIA: Is there a bank machine nearby?

CINDY: There's a TD on this side of the street, right by the front door, five steps to the west. You can't miss it. And there's a Bank of Commerce on the other side of the street, on the corner.

SYLVIA: I'll be back in a few moments.

CINDY: Great. Cool. Okay.

SYLVIA: All right.

(SYLVIA leaves. CINDY goes to the answering machine. Rewinds the message.)

HOLLY: She is not moving into this apartment.

CINDY: Where's the rent.

HOLLY: I thought we were going to decide on this together.

CINDY: Where's the rent Holly.

HOLLY: I'll pay the rent.

CINDY: Now. For right now. Where's the rent. I covered you for last month when you know I can't, you know the situation I'm in right now and I covered you.

HOLLY: Look ...

CINDY: I know you're good for it, I know you are, but right now we have a total stranger who is going to give us nine hundred dollars cash. You got a better idea, you got nine hundred dollars you're going to magically pull out of thin air, you better do it quick.

(CINDY rewinds the last message.)

HOLLY: All I need is to get this job and ...

(CINDY plays the last message.)

LANDLORD: *(On tape.)* Okay, girls, listen—I talked to my lawyer, and it turns out I can evict you for non-payment at any point after the fifteenth. Now I ... I don't want to do this you understand ...

(CINDY turns the answering machine off. She paces the room thinking.)

HOLLY: Just relax, tomorrow we'll ...

CINDY: Holly I love you shut up.

HOLLY: It's only ...

CINDY: You know what you're gonna do? When she gets back here, you are gonna get on your bike and you're gonna hustle …

HOLLY: I'm in the middle of rendering.

CINDY: Holly, please. Please. Okay? Give him the money, apologize profusely for the delay, pay him, and tell him that the rest of the money we can get to him by the end of the month. All right? All right?

HOLLY: But …

CINDY: Holly.

HOLLY: All right.

(There is a knock at the door.)

CINDY: Come in.

(SYLVIA returns.)

SYLVIA: *(Offstage.)* Hello.

CINDY: Come on up.

(SYLVIA enters.)

SYLVIA: I'm sorry it took so long.

CINDY: No, that was very fast. It was fine.

SYLVIA: Who do I …

(CINDY puts out her hand. SYLVIA hands the money to CINDY. CINDY hands the money over to HOLLY.)

CINDY: You're gonna love having a bank machine right by the front door. It's a curse, but you'll love it.

SYLVIA: It should be all there. I haven't counted it yet but …

HOLLY: Don't worry about it.

SYLVIA: I'm not worried about it, I just haven't counted it yet.

HOLLY: Okifine.

(HOLLY grabs her coat.)

Do me a favour. If a dialogue box appears saying "Render Fireplace" could you hit "enter"?

CINDY: You got it.

(HOLLY notices that SYLVIA is staring at her.)

HOLLY: See ya.

(She leaves.)

CINDY: Now were you going to move stuff in later today, or … Sylvia? Do you have a lot of stuff to move in, or …

SYLVIA: Uh no.

CINDY: Okay, well, you can use the bed that's in there already. If you need pillows or covers or anything I'm sure we could dig something up.

SYLVIA: Okay.

CINDY: So when are you gonna move the rest of your stuff in?

SYLVIA: What?

CINDY: When are you going to move the rest of your stuff in here?

SYLVIA: I don't know.

CINDY: Is there a particular day?

SYLVIA: No.

CINDY: Well, let us know and we'll give you a hand. All right?

SYLVIA: All right.

(CINDY puts on her coat, grabs her bike.)

CINDY: Great. So, keys on the fridge. Make yourself at home. All the stuff in the cupboard next to the fridge is mine. You need some food, go for it, don't even ask. There's a grocery store ... Sylvia?

SYLVIA: Yes.

CINDY: You okay?

SYLVIA: Yes. I'm fine.

CINDY: Really?

SYLVIA: Yes, I just ... I'm fine.

CINDY: Okay well, I've got to head out, but if you need to talk—*(She motions to herself.)*—okay?

SYLVIA: All right.

(CINDY leaves.)

All right.

(CINDY leaves. SYLVIA breathes deeply. She opens up her leather case, and her cell phone. Hits a speed dial button.)

Sarah. It's me. I know.

(She breathes in and out.)

Hold on.

(She rifles through her files, pulls out a number of them and her laptop. She takes one last deep breath.)

Ready? Go to sequence 127. 178,546.98. I'm sorry I didn't get this to you earlier. I came downtown to pick up the EHTs at Kinkos, and I saw my husband with another woman. I can't talk about it right now. The meeting at 4:30, I can't make it. Tell them I had a family emergency. No, I can't talk about it right now, I have to go. I have to go. Bye. Bye.

(Music. The image of a window, the point of view from within the house, looking out over a street in the Bathurst and St. Claire area is projected.)

JORDAN: *(Offstage.)* Should we wait or is it just you and me?

(JORDAN enters with a bowl of sauce, a wooden spoon, and a can of seasoning.)

SYLVIA: Sorry?

JORDAN: Is she coming straight home from school or …?

SYLVIA: No, she's got soccer practice.

JORDAN: So I said, "Look, that was then, this is now. Maybe Macintosh can afford to have a twenty-seven-month development cycle but we can't." Taste this.

SYLVIA: More salt.

JORDAN: I'm not using more salt.

SYLVIA: Jordan, you asked my opinion.

JORDAN: Fine.

(JORDAN goes to the kitchen.)

(Offstage.) Trilinear filtering, Bump mapping, texture compression. That's the competition, okay? I mean, we can spend the next six-month cycle …

(JORDAN returns from the kitchen with the bowl.)

… shopping around our second-rate, crappy-looking, 16 bit graphics to OEMs, or we can get … are you listening to me or do you need some quiet time, or what.

SYLVIA: I'm listening to you. Keep talking.

JORDAN: Or we can get our act together, clean up the Open GL rendering with a new driver release, and put the rest of the money into transform and lighting. That's the future.

SYLVIA: What'd they say?

JORDAN: Well, I'm not … when you're not a programmer … they just don't take my musings as seriously as they used to.

(He makes her taste the sauce. She motions to him that it is perfect.)

SYLVIA: You just watch. One day you're gonna find your idea's being used but you don't get the credit.

JORDAN: Okay okay.

SYLVIA: Look, you can dismiss me, you can do whatever you like, but I see this kind of thing all the time.

JORDAN: I know.

SYLVIA: What's that guy's name, Steven …

JORDAN: Steven?

SYLVIA: That guy there, with the red beard, balding, with the glasses.

JORDAN: Marretti.

(SYLVIA stretches.)

SYLVIA: You just watch your back with him.

JORDAN: Sure, okay.

SYLVIA: I'm telling you, watch your …

(To emphasize her point she raises her arm above her head. She experiences a severe pain.)

JORDAN: You all right?

SYLVIA: Yeah, I just … I forgot.

JORDAN: How're you feeling.

SYLVIA: Little nauseous.

JORDAN: Back rub?

SYLVIA: No.

JORDAN: Tummy rub?

SYLVIA: No. Thank you.

JORDAN: Keep your arms down okay? You want to grab something, get something off a shelf, you call me.

SYLVIA: All right.

JORDAN: Anyway, the upshot is that they want me to do the Comdex show again.

(JORDAN goes to the kitchen. SYLVIA goes to the window. She looks outside.)

(Offstage.) Thing is, the date of the show is around the time you'll be going in for the testing, so I don't know, what do you think? Honey?

(He steps out of the kitchen with a tea cloth over his shoulder and a pair of oven mitts.)

Honey?

SYLVIA: Could I get you to hold me?

(He holds her.)

JORDAN: How's this.

SYLVIA: Fine.

JORDAN: One thing you must know … two, two things you must know.

SYLVIA: What's that.

JORDAN: You're going to be fine. I will always be here for you.

SYLVIA: All right.

JORDAN: Hungry?

SYLVIA: Yeah, I have to eat.

JORDAN: Dinner'll be ready in ten minutes. And then after dinner, how about we go out to the Beaches, take a stroll, look into some shops, get an ice cream? Would you like that?

SYLVIA: I would like that very much.

(JORDAN kisses her. Walks back towards the kitchen. Stops.)

JORDAN: Do you put the … is it onions, then ackee then salt fish, or is it onion, salt fish, ackee?

SYLVIA: I don't think it matters.

JORDAN: You're gonna have to come in, check things out.

SYLVIA: *(With a Jamaican accent.)* All right.

JORDAN: *(Offstage, mocking her accent.)* All right.

(He leaves. Projection of the window fades. Music. SYLVIA takes out three pill bottles. She swallows a pill from each. She puts her headphones on and presses "play" on her portable CD player. She lays back and closes her eyes. CINDY enters with the "Room For Rent" sign. She puts it away and takes off her jacket. Looks at SYLVIA. Puts her bike away. CINDY makes a noise that disturbs SYLVIA.)

CINDY: Sorry.

SYLVIA: That's all right.

CINDY: So … how did you find out about our place?

SYLVIA: I beg your pardon?

CINDY: How did you find out about the apartment.

SYLVIA: I saw the sign in the door.

CINDY: Oh, right. Uh, I should just warn you, all this wine belongs to Holly. She doesn't mind if you take one of the newer Ontario wines, just make sure you replace it within twenty-four hours.

This bottle, you do not touch. Make sure you memorize the label so that even if you're pissed out of your mind, you never open this bottle.

SYLVIA: All right.

CINDY: Oh, and I was going to tell you this earlier, and I didn't, but I should have; I'm actually going to be moving out in about a month and a half. There's lots of time before we have to find someone. I have a couple of friends who could come in here, they're totally cool. If you know someone, that's great too. It's going to be a shared decision. Okay?

SYLVIA: Okay.

CINDY: I know I should have mentioned this earlier, and I feel bad ...

SYLVIA: Don't feel bad. It's all right.

CINDY: It's going to be a shared decision.

SYLVIA: I understand.

CINDY: Okay. Oh, and uh, I guess now is as good a time as any to tell you, we got mice, and we got cockroaches. It's Bathurst and Bloor, we live above a restaurant, we've tried everything, there's nothing we can do about it.

SYLVIA: Is that it?

CINDY: Yes, that's it.

SYLVIA: Good.

CINDY: Want some wine?

SYLVIA: No thank you.

CINDY: Okay. I'll leave you alone now. Bye.

(CINDY pulls a bottle of wine out of the wine rack, goes to her darkroom. SYLVIA pulls out her cell phone.)

SYLVIA: Hey it's me. Dinner's in the green plastic container. Hope school went well today. I know you're going to Margaret's this weekend but I probably won't see you before you leave. I'll be away for the weekend. Give me a call on my cell when you get this message, and I'll tell you more. Oh and if you happen to see your father, tell him, ask him if ... if he's ... nothing. Forget it. Bye.

(SYLVIA looks around. Sees the answering machine. She presses "play." As the messages play, SYLVIA looks through everything she can in the apartment.)

MARY: *(Voiceover.)* Hi, this is Mary from *Now* magazine for Cindy. I just want to confirm that we are going to receive your prints before midnight. Okay. Thank you. Bye.

(Beep.)

MRS. SHORT: *(Voiceover.)* Hello, I'm calling for a Ms. Holly Dumont. It is Mrs. Short from Revenue Canada. If she could give me a call, as soon as possible, thank you.

(Beep.)

ARLENE: Honey, I totally forgot to call the woman about renting the hall. I'm sorry, I dropped the ball. When I get back from Vancouver, I am going to be so focused. I swear. I can't talk right now. Love you. Bye.

(Beep.)

JEAN-MARC: Holly. *J'ai un petit poème pour toi.* Okay. *Tu es la plaie et le couteau, chu la victime et le bourreau.* Okay, thank you. Bye bye.

(Beep.)

JORDAN: *(Voiceover.)* Hello. Holly. You there? Pick up the phone if you're there. Okay well …

(HOLLY's voice comes in.)

HOLLY: *(Voiceover.)* Hey baby …

(Beep.)

LANDLORD: *(Voiceover.)* Okay, girls, listen …

(SYLVIA rewinds the tape.

Beep.)

JORDAN: *(Voiceover.)* Hello. Holly. You there? Pick up the phone if you're there. Okay well …

(HOLLY's voice comes in.)

HOLLY: *(Voiceover.)* Hey baby …

(Beep. The front door opens. SYLVIA shuts off the answering machine. HOLLY enters with her bike.)

You have a car? Yo.

SYLVIA: Can I help you?

HOLLY: You have a car?

SYLVIA: Yes I do. Why?

HOLLY: When you park your car, make sure to look behind you before you open your door. I almost got clipped by some Rosedale bitch.

SYLVIA: Do you have to use that language?

HOLLY: I beg your pardon.

SYLVIA: Language. Do you have to use that word.

HOLLY: No, I don't, but some rich bitch almost killed my ass, I'm sorry if it offends you.

(She looks at the computer. CINDY didn't press the button to render "Fireplace.")

Gee Cindy. Thanks a lot.

(She presses "enter.")

Any calls for me?

SYLVIA: What?

HOLLY: I'm expecting a call. Any calls for me.

SYLVIA: No.

HOLLY: Really?

SYLVIA: Yes.

HOLLY: You have a problem with me?

SYLVIA: What?

HOLLY: If you have a problem with me, let's get it out in the open.

SYLVIA: I do not have a problem with you.

HOLLY: I just get this vibe from you that you have a problem with me.

SYLVIA: I do not.

HOLLY: Okay.

(HOLLY starts scratching her skin. SYLVIA opens her laptop, pulls out some files and goes to work.)

Do you find it dry in here?

SYLVIA: No.

HOLLY: My skin's itchy.

SYLVIA: Get a humidifier.

HOLLY: Well, we've got one on the furnace, but I don't think it's working.

SYLVIA: Oh.

HOLLY: Do you know how those things work?

SYLVIA: No I do not.

HOLLY: All right.

(SYLVIA's computer crashes.)

SYLVIA: Oh damn.

HOLLY: You okay?

SYLVIA: I'm fine.

HOLLY: Laptop crash?

SYLVIA: It's fine, I …

(SYLVIA reaches to turn the laptop off.)

HOLLY: Don't do that. Don't do that. You could corrupt your hard drive. Here. May I?

(SYLVIA lets her touch her laptop.)

I work with Macs all the time. I got it. This guy I'm seeing now. He's a big computer guy, works for a big video card company, and he was saying to me that, here we go, hold on, he was saying to me that the Mac is a superior platform, wait. Okay, I see. But sometimes you can run into completely modal dialogues like this, that don't let you do anything else at all. There. Try it now.

(SYLVIA starts working again.)

How is it.

SYLVIA: Fine. Thank you.

(HOLLY puts her hands on SYLVIA's shoulders to say "you're welcome." SYLVIA lets her.)

HOLLY: The moment you get OS 10, your Mac is gonna rock, but until that happens, try to keep a close watch on your extensions.

SYLVIA: Sure.

HOLLY: *Puhd'problème.*

(HOLLY goes back to work.)

SYLVIA: What do you do exactly?

HOLLY: What was that?

SYLVIA: What do you do. For a living.

(HOLLY pulls out a business card.)

HOLLY: Graphic artist. I don't actually have a position anywhere. Yet. What I'm doing right now is putting together a portfolio of my computer graphics work.

SYLVIA: I see.

HOLLY: I'm applying to the new paper, whatever it's called …

SYLVIA: The *Post?*

HOLLY: Yeah, yeah. As far as I'm concerned, it's a fascist rag in a sea of fascist rags, but a girl's gotta eat, right? So.

SYLVIA: And what does your boyfriend do?

HOLLY: Well, he's not exactly my boyfriend. He's just this guy I'm kinda seeing.

SYLVIA: All right.

HOLLY: I just came out of a really, bad … I'm not really looking for a boyfriend right now so …

SYLVIA: Does he know this?

HOLLY: He better.

SYLVIA: I see.

HOLLY: Besides, he's married.

SYLVIA: Oh is he.

HOLLY: Yeah, I know. I'm pulling such a Monica Lewinsky it's not funny. But I didn't plan on it. It just kinda happened.

SYLVIA: How did you two meet?

(CINDY enters sucking a lollipop, with a bridal magazine in her hand.)

CINDY: What about this?

HOLLY: What.

CINDY: For a dress.

HOLLY: You already have a dress.

CINDY: Just tell me what you think.

HOLLY: It's very frilly.

CINDY: Frilly?

HOLLY: That can be a good thing.

CINDY: What do you think?

SYLVIA: What am I looking at?

CINDY: Wedding dress.

SYLVIA: You're getting married?

(CINDY shows SYLVIA her engagement ring.)

CINDY: Now I was thinking this one, or this. Without the head thing.

SYLVIA: It's fine I suppose.

HOLLY: You've already got a wedding dress, calm down.

CINDY: My mother hates it, my sister hates it …

HOLLY: It's your wedding. It's your day, tell them it's none of their damn business.

CINDY: Yeah, sure, right, okay, yeah, sure.

HOLLY: I'm serious. Don't let it get to you. You let it get to you, you stress about it. You stress about it, your immune system shuts down. Why do you think you've got that urinary tract infection again …

CINDY: Shut up.

HOLLY: It's true.

CINDY: *(To SYLVIA.)* She's—

HOLLY: Listen to me, you cannot control how people feel. You can't. You can only control your actions. Not how people feel about them. Do you like the dress? Wear the dress.

CINDY: Okay, I totally know how this is going to make me sound, but just bear with me, all right? Now, honestly, you don't think it makes my hips too …

HOLLY: Your hips are beautiful.

CINDY: Yeah yeah.

HOLLY: Now I'm going to smack you—

CINDY: *(Simultaneously with HOLLY's next line.)* You have always had the great body. I …

HOLLY: *(Simultaneously with CINDY.)*—so hard! What are you talking about!

SYLVIA: Please! I … I have a headache. I'm sorry. I just …

CINDY: Would you like a Tylenol?

SYLVIA: No it's …

CINDY: It's no bother.

(CINDY goes into the kitchen. SYLVIA goes back to work. HOLLY goes to work and looks over at SYLVIA on occasion. CINDY returns with the pills.)

Here you go.

(SYLVIA gently holds CINDY's hand.)

SYLVIA: Cranberry juice.

CINDY: I beg your pardon?

SYLVIA: For your … problem. Get a two-litre bottle of cranberry juice, not the cocktail, it has to be the juice. Get one of those plastic containers with the spout, keep it filled to the brim with juice at all times and drink from it all day for two days straight. If it hasn't gone away by Monday, call your doctor.

CINDY: Are you serious.

SYLVIA: I am very serious.

(CINDY grabs her bike.)

HOLLY: Where you going?

CINDY: Grocery store.

HOLLY: Pick me up a pack of cigarettes while you're there.

(HOLLY scrounges through a jar full of change.)

CINDY: I'll get it.

HOLLY: I can get it, don't worry.

CINDY: I'm not carrying six dollars worth of pennies. I'll get it, you'll owe me.

HOLLY: Okay.

(CINDY kisses HOLLY's forehead. She carries her bike outside.)

I'm gonna start some coffee. Want some?

SYLVIA: I, uh …

HOLLY: Tell you what, I'll put it on, when it's ready, you decide then, all right?

SYLVIA: All right.

(HOLLY goes to the kitchen.)

So tell me …

HOLLY: *(Offstage.)* Yes.

(SYLVIA decides not to ask the question she wants to ask.)

SYLVIA: May I take a look at what you're working on?

HOLLY: *(Offstage.)* Sure, well, okay. Hold on.

(SYLVIA looks at Holly's computer screen. HOLLY steps out of the kitchen with a bag of ground coffee.)

SYLVIA: Is this your work?

HOLLY: Yeah, but you can't really see it cause it's rendering right now. But I can show you my CG portfolio if you like.

SYLVIA: CG?

HOLLY: Computer graphics. Sorry.

SYLVIA: Okay.

(HOLLY pulls out a portfolio that was tucked away in a corner.)

HOLLY: This is all Corel Draw stuff here. Ray Dream 3D work here.

SYLVIA: Okay.

HOLLY: I was trying to do something on the whole matrilineal nature of the Iroquois. I thought it was very clever at the time.

(SYLVIA moves to a large painting with a cover on it.)

SYLVIA: What's this over here?

HOLLY: I'll do that. It's okay.

(HOLLY pulls off the cover.)

SYLVIA: Oh.

HOLLY: This is from a series of paintings I did on the whole thing about how in Japan, they outlawed the birth control pill so that doctors could make a fortune performing abortions. Thousands of women die every year from the procedure and here in the West we don't say anything about it because no one in the women's movement wants to risk giving anti-abortionists any kind of ammunition. The politics of it are ... problematic to say the least. I really enjoy that.

SYLVIA: What's this over here?

(SYLVIA picks up the ceremonial knife she was looking at earlier.)

HOLLY: Don't touch that.

SYLVIA: All right.

(HOLLY grabs it.)

HOLLY: It's very sharp. In Senegal they use something like this for female circumcision. I was trying to ... it's not an exact replica but I was trying to do something on the whole fear of female sexual power thing. How some of the older generation of women are perpetuating the ritual. It was a part of a larger thing. Anyway.

SYLVIA: So is all this ... do you sell your work, or ...

HOLLY: No no. Well I ... had one exhibition, about a year ago. Last ... April? I think?

SYLVIA: I see.

HOLLY: I believe the most generous review I received was from Deirdre Hanna who declared my work profoundly naive.

SYLVIA: Really.

HOLLY: Ironically for me, the same reviews that ended my career as an artist in Toronto caught the attention of an American film producer who was here to shoot a made-for-TV movie about a crazed twenty-something artist who falls in love with a married man and then proceeds to try and kill his wife.

(SYLVIA laughs.)

There's this scene in the film where the artist burns to death surrounded by her artwork and they wanted to buy a whole heap of my stuff for fifty thousand dollars. Fifty thousand dollars so they could film it going up in flames. I could tell you about all the conversations I had with my friends. Late-night disputations on integrity, about how I would never allow my art to be used by an American to reinforce stereotypical Madonna–whore complex crap. I would love to be able to tell you that I told him to take a long walk off a short pier, but I did not. No, I took the money, I bought that computer, that bike, supplies. I went to the Turks and Caicos. I went to Spain. I gave some to my parents. Friends. I moved into this palatial "House of All Sorts." I bought a bottle of Maristol Beaujolais 1976. I did everything I could to get that money out of my bank account and now it's gone. All of it. It took a while but now it is all gone. I still don't have a career as an artist in Toronto, but I feel *great.*

SYLVIA: Good for you.

HOLLY: Some time, before you die, you have to give yourself the opportunity to blow fifty thousand dollars.

SYLVIA: Really.

HOLLY: It is absolutely liberating.

SYLVIA: Thing is, you can't really tell when you're going to die, can you. I mean, who knows, you could always be murdered by the woman having an affair with your husband.

HOLLY: … Oh right. Yeah. Exactly.

(CINDY enters with juice and cigarettes.)

CINDY: Here we go.

HOLLY: They didn't have any Player's Light—? I mean thank you so much Cindy for everything you've done for me ever.

CINDY: You're welcome.

(The phone rings.)

HOLLY: You going to answer that?

CINDY: I'm busy.

(CINDY goes to the kitchen. HOLLY answers the phone.)

HOLLY: Hello? Hey you. I'm almost done. I just need to do a couple more images, put 'em on a Zip disk, fire them off to Kinkos. Where are you? No. Okay. Lay it on me.

(HOLLY returns.)

Really? Congratulations honey! That's amazing. Oh. Uh, sure, okay. No no. I uh, I have to be back here for Monday morning, but that's about it. When? I can do it. Sure can. What are you going to tell your wife? Really? Okay well, no hey that's … I know some very nice Auberges right on St. Denis where we can bring our own wine and everything. Okay. I gotta pack. Okay. Give me some time to finish this up here, then you give me a call when you're all set. Okay? Okay. Bye. Okay bye. What? … I love you too. Yeah, okay. No you hang up. No you hang up. But it was my turn last time. Okay. Bye. Bye. Bye.

(HOLLY gives a shriek or shout of elation.)

Eeeeuuuooo!

(CINDY enters.)

CINDY: What's going on.

HOLLY: I'm going to Montreal!

CINDY: Get out!

HOLLY: He just sealed some account with a company in Florida, and he wants to celebrate so he's flying me to Montreal!

CINDY: He's flying you to Montreal?

HOLLY: I am a kept woman.

(CINDY summons up her irony.)

CINDY: Good for you.

HOLLY: I've never been a kept woman before.

CINDY: When are you coming back?

HOLLY: Sunday night.

CINDY: What's he gonna tell his wife.

HOLLY: She's away for the weekend and so is his daughter.

CINDY: Oh really.

HOLLY: Yeah, well, what can I say, I'm a hottie. Now if you'll excuse me, I've got some rendering to do, then I gotta grab a quick shower …

CINDY: Let me get my laundry off the rack first.

HOLLY: Then you are gonna help me pick out some "kept woman in Montreal" outfits.

CINDY: *O joie o blis.*

(HOLLY goes back to work. CINDY goes upstairs.)

HOLLY: Sylvia.

SYLVIA: Yes?

HOLLY: Can I ask you a question?

SYLVIA: Yes?

HOLLY: What has two thumbs, speaks French, and is the sexiest thing on the planet?

SYLVIA: I don't …

(HOLLY uses her thumbs to point to herself.)

HOLLY: *Tabarnac, c'est moi!!*

(She goes back to work.)

SYLVIA: How did you two meet?

HOLLY: Hahn?

(Lights up on JORDAN.)

SYLVIA: This man you're running off with, how did you two meet.

JORDAN: … as a major initiative to bring a dramatic price/performance discontinuity to the visualization market.

HOLLY: At Comdex.

SYLVIA: Comdex.

(The painting changes to a sketch of a personal computer.)

HOLLY: It's a computer expo.

SYLVIA: I know what it is.

JORDAN: Not only can it achieve high speeds in our stunningly beautiful 16 bit mode …

SYLVIA: Did he approach you or …

HOLLY: I'm sorry.

JORDAN: … but, as you will see, there is not a single drop in frame rate in full 32 bit colour.

SYLVIA: Did he come on to you or …

JORDAN: Would you like to try?

HOLLY: I'm sorry?

JORDAN: We have a demo set up, would you like to try?

HOLLY: Uh no. No thank you.

JORDAN: Don't tell me, let me guess. Graphic design student.

HOLLY: Could you turn this way please.

JORDAN: Beg your pardon?

HOLLY: Could you just turn your body over this way. Now talk to me again.

JORDAN: Okay.

HOLLY: You're not talking.

JORDAN: I have no idea what to say.

HOLLY: 32 bit rendering. Tell me about it.

JORDAN: Uh yes. Uh, the new 128 chipset will incorporate 32 bit graphics technology into new desktop systems and accelerate product time-to-market. Is he gone?

HOLLY: Yeah.

JORDAN: Ex-boyfriend?

HOLLY: Almost.

JORDAN: I see.

HOLLY: You ever break up with someone and they just don't want to take no for an answer?

JORDAN: Once. Long time ago.

HOLLY: What happened?

JORDAN: I married her. Badum ching. That's not true. That was a joke. I'm joking. I love my wife.

HOLLY: Yeah?

JORDAN: Yes I do. I love my wife. I do.

HOLLY: All right.

JORDAN: So who's this guy. What's his name.

HOLLY: Jean-Marc.

JORDAN: French guy.

HOLLY: *Mais bien sûr.*

JORDAN: Things didn't go well.

HOLLY: He's a psychopath.

JORDAN: That's too bad.

HOLLY: Sort of. It's also kinda what I fell in love with in the first place. You get what you pay for I guess.

JORDAN: I guess.

HOLLY: So tell me about your wife.

JORDAN: Sorry?

HOLLY: Tell me about your wife.

JORDAN: I love my wife.

HOLLY: That's like the third time you've said that.

JORDAN: Because "like" it's true.

HOLLY: All right.

JORDAN: How old are you?

HOLLY: Why?

JORDAN: How old are you?

HOLLY: Age means nothing.

JORDAN: Really.

HOLLY: We know different lyrics to different pop songs, and we buy different products that are marketed to us with different tag lines. That's it.

JORDAN: Well la-de-da.

HOLLY: Well la-de-dee, la-de-da.

JORDAN: So, what are you looking for here?

HOLLY: How do you mean?

JORDAN: Are you looking for a graphics accelerator, or …

HOLLY: Open GL card.

JORDAN: Ah. I see.

HOLLY: Have any?

JORDAN: Yes we do.

HOLLY: Let's see 'em.

JORDAN: The Fire GL is our top of the line …

HOLLY: Why do you do that?

JORDAN: What?

HOLLY: With your voice. You go into this kind of …

JORDAN: It's from … I say this stuff a lot and …

HOLLY: Just talk to me. Like you are now. The way you speak normally is very nice. Just talk to me.

JORDAN: Our Fire GL card comes with a full Open GL ICD and … how's that?

HOLLY: Now you're trying to be sexy. It doesn't work when you try.

JORDAN: Our Fire GL card comes with a full ICD.

(She puts her hand on his chest.)

HOLLY: That was very nice.

JORDAN: Thank you.

(He takes her hand off his chest, but he takes his time letting go of it.)

HOLLY: I hope your wife appreciates that she has such a sexy-voiced man at home.

JORDAN: Listen, you gonna buy a card or you gonna sit here and talk all day. I got a business to run.

HOLLY: So tell me again about the 32 bit rendering?

(HOLLY stands very close to JORDAN.)

JORDAN: The 32 bit rendering on the Rage 128 …

HOLLY: What?

JORDAN: I uhm. I have to make a call.

HOLLY: Okay.

JORDAN: But I'm sure someone here can help you.

HOLLY: Okay.

JORDAN: Excuse me.

HOLLY: Could I … do you have a card? Business card?

JORDAN: Sure.

HOLLY: May I …

JORDAN: Yes.

(He turns to leave, he stops and turns back)

If you … have any questions, please, don't hesitate to call.

HOLLY: Okay.

(JORDAN turns away. He is not pleased with himself.)

CINDY: *(Offstage.)* You can use the shower now.

HOLLY: I gotta go.

(HOLLY goes to the computer. The image of a computer crossfades to HOLLY's painting.)

SYLVIA: Uh …

HOLLY: I'll be there in a second.

(CINDY enters with her clothes and a bottle of cranberry juice. She points to the couch.)

CINDY: Can I …

SYLVIA: Sure, Uh …

(SYLVIA grabs her things. CINDY sits on the couch, and folds clothes.)

CINDY: I'll just …

SYLVIA: I'm sorry, I …

CINDY: I'll just take this part here.

HOLLY: Don't mess with anything.

CINDY: Can I get my e-mail?

HOLLY: You can get your e-mail and that's it.

(HOLLY leaves.)

CINDY: You must have a lot of work to do?

SYLVIA: I'm sorry, what did you ask me?

CINDY: Work. I see you got a lot of work there to do.

SYLVIA: Uhm … Yes. Yes I do.

CINDY: If you want, you can use the desk in my room upstairs if you like. It's quieter and …

SYLVIA: I'm fine. It's okay.

CINDY: You know, you … can feel free to make yourself totally at home here. You know that right?

SYLVIA: Yes.

CINDY: Tell you what: I just have to finish off a few more prints and drop them off. Then I was thinking about renting a movie. Whadaya say.

SYLVIA: Fine.

CINDY: Comedy or action. No romance films.

SYLVIA: That's fine.

CINDY: No Julia Roberts …

SYLVIA: That's fine.

CINDY: She just works my last nerve.

SYLVIA: So. Holly was telling me about how she met … uh … what's his name again?

CINDY: Jordan?

SYLVIA: Yes.

CINDY: Pretty wild huhn.

SYLVIA: It's …

CINDY: What?

SYLVIA: He's … he's … he's … he's a married man.

CINDY: Yeah I know.

(The painting becomes the page of a letter.)

SYLVIA: Doesn't that … it's …

CINDY: Okay, can I tell you something.

SYLVIA: Go right ahead.

CINDY: When I first heard about this whole thing, I tried reasoning with her. I did. Especially after I met him.

SYLVIA: Really.

CINDY: You have to see this guy. You really do. He's ... it's like he's one of these jerks who has amassed a certain amount of material wealth in the new economy, right? I'm sure he's got some trophy wife that he met when she was a model or a cheerleader, and he keeps her at home, raising his children. And now that she doesn't look so young, and the breasts don't point in the same direction any more, suddenly he wants to get a little action on the side. Right? And Holly? Everything is a little easy for her, right? It's not a real commitment, right? Eventually she's gonna want him to leave his wife, and he's gonna lie and tell her he's so close to getting divorced blah blah blah. That's what happens right? It's ancient, it's primordial. Blah de blah blah. So as a friend, I can tell her what ... I can say things to get her thinking more cynically. Getting her to focus on what she really has to deal with inside, and I think I've convinced her. I think I'm making headway. I think I've got her on my side. Then suddenly, out of nowhere, she writes him this letter, and ...

SYLVIA: Letter?

(HOLLY is stage right with the letter. As HOLLY reads, SYLVIA takes the letter from her hand. Halfway through the letter, light comes up on stage left, where JORDAN stands.)

HOLLY: I write to you as a way of allowing a gentle resolution to a most enjoyable experience with a very handsome married man. I thank you for your help with my "petit problème" and I am seriously looking forward to more information on what I am sure is an excellent GL card. My last one has caused me nothing but frustration and torment, and I am curious to know ... how yours will perform.

(JORDAN enters with his jacket on. He's tired.)

JORDAN: Sorry I'm late honey. We had a staff meeting that went a little late and the 401 was a mess. Have you eaten? What? What's the matter?

SYLVIA: I found this letter. I was doing the laundry. I found this letter.

(She holds up the note.)

JORDAN: Yeah.

SYLVIA: Do you have any idea where it came from?

JORDAN: Well what does it say?

(She hands it to him. He reads it.)

Hmm. That's odd.

SYLVIA: What's odd.

JORDAN: Is this it? Is this the only page?

SYLVIA: Why?

JORDAN: Well it is one page in what was obviously a much longer letter. Is there another page?

SYLVIA: No.

JORDAN: I mean, it looks like it's the second page in a series or something.

SYLVIA: Do you know who wrote it?

JORDAN: It could be my secretary's handwriting, but then again it could be … I don't know …

SYLVIA: How did it get into your possession?

(JORDAN flips the paper over.)

JORDAN: I used it as a piece of scrap paper to write a phone number. You think that the married guy, in the letter, you think that's me.

SYLVIA: I don't know what to think.

JORDAN: It's a piece of scrap paper. They have a pile at work of scrap paper. Whoever wrote this, they obviously thought that it deserved to be used as scrap paper. I picked it up. I used it. It's … you know.

SYLVIA: Fine.

JORDAN: Come on. I'm gonna, what, keep one page out of a letter from my mistress, write a phone number on the back and then keep it laying around?

SYLVIA: That's fine, I just wanted an answer.

JORDAN: I mean, I can understand how you could make that mistake, but please. I don't see my name here. I don't see any names. I mean …

SYLVIA: Go make some food.

JORDAN: I mean if you're really serious about this I can take it into work and ask around …

SYLVIA: I don't care. I'm hungry now. Go make some food.

(SYLVIA leaves.)

JORDAN: All right. Okay. How are you. How was your day.

(JORDAN crumples up the letter and tosses it across the room. A phone rings; we are in an office voice mail system.)

VOICE: *(Voiceover.)*For the company directory press one.

(We hear HOLLY press "two.")

(Voiceover.) If you know the extension—

(The sound of three phone keys is heard. The phone rings. It picks up. Light up on HOLLY stage left, phone to her ear. She is distraught.)

HOLLY: Hey there.

JORDAN: I'm glad you called.

HOLLY: Can we uh …

JORDAN: What's the matter.

HOLLY: Can we uh …

JORDAN: You want to get together?

HOLLY: Could we?

JORDAN: I'll make lunch reservations for two at Bombay Palace.

HOLLY: I really need to talk to you.

JORDAN: What is it?

HOLLY: I can't talk right now.

JORDAN: Is he there?

HOLLY: Yeah.

JORDAN: Bombay Palace at two, all right?

HOLLY: All right.

(HOLLY hangs up. Music.

Lights up on JORDAN in the restaurant. He is reading the paper, making marks on the page with his pen. HOLLY enters.)

So sorry I'm late.

JORDAN: No, it's okay.

HOLLY: This the menu?

JORDAN: Relax, sit back. There's no rush. You okay?

HOLLY: No. I'm not.

JORDAN: Problems with your man?

HOLLY: He. It's just so draining. You know? You don't mind if I smoke do you?

(JORDAN shakes his head and HOLLY lights up.)

It's like … we started off this relationship very … we were very reckless, and it was all passion and anger, and that's okay when you're just starting out, but …

JORDAN: Is it …

HOLLY: I came to Toronto because I wanted to do a show. I wanted to get enough work together to do a show. Fine. Suddenly he wants to come to Toronto because *he* wants to do a show. Fine. We get an apartment. Cool. I'm doing all this stuff, making connections, I get in tight with Andrew Harwood at the Mercer Union, I'm getting focused, putting together my installations, sculptures, everything. He's sitting on his ass, drinking, smoking up, bitching about how he doesn't have any money but he won't go out and get a job. His mother is on welfare, renting a one-room apartment in St. Jovite, he's begging her to send him money for smokes. The only thing he can possibly allow himself to say about my work is that it's insincere. And suddenly he's wondering why I've stopped sleeping with him! He can't figure out why the hell I can't stand to hear the sound of his voice. I just ... I want him out. I want him out of the apartment. I want him out of my life. I want him out.

JORDAN: Need any help convincing him? I'm serious.

HOLLY: What are you talking about?

JORDAN: I was just thinking that if you had someone standing next to you, it might give your words a little more authority, that's all.

HOLLY: You'd do that for me?

JORDAN: How big is he?

HOLLY: How big is he?

JORDAN: I mean, is he gonna open up some kung fu on my ass or something?

HOLLY: No.

JORDAN: Jiu-jitsu, tae kwon do ...

HOLLY: No jiu-jitsu, no tae kwon do.

JORDAN: All right, well, how about this, I finish work at 5:00, I can be at your place at 5:45?

HOLLY: What about your ...

JORDAN: Don't worry about it.

HOLLY: Okay.

JORDAN: I'd have to leave at some point. I couldn't stay.

HOLLY: Right. All right.

JORDAN: Consider the situation solved.

HOLLY: Jordan ...

JORDAN: It's done. Put it out of your mind.

HOLLY: ... you're saving my life.

JORDAN: Yeah yeah yeah.

HOLLY: No really. I mean it. Thank you.

(She holds his hand.)

JORDAN: I feel more testosterone in my system than I have in years. It's great. Thank you.

(He takes her cigarette and takes a long drag from it.)

HOLLY: So.

JORDAN: So.

HOLLY: What about you.

JORDAN: What about me.

HOLLY: How are you doing?

JORDAN: Fine.

HOLLY: Just fine.

JORDAN: Just fine.

HOLLY: You're in a relationship right now, aren't you?

JORDAN: Yes I am.

HOLLY: How's it going?

JORDAN: It's okay.

HOLLY: Really.

JORDAN: Uh huhn.

HOLLY: Why don't you talk about it? You never talk about your relationship, it's always me.

JORDAN: Is that a problem?

HOLLY: Well, I just … I like, start to feel like I'm this crazy mad woman that fascinates you or something.

JORDAN: You are.

HOLLY: Well now it's your turn.

JORDAN: What would you like to know?

HOLLY: Did you tell your wife that you were going to meet me for lunch?

JORDAN: No I did not.

HOLLY: Are you going to?

JORDAN: No I am not.

HOLLY: That's not good.

JORDAN: No it is not.

HOLLY: You two fight at all?

JORDAN: Yes we do.

HOLLY: Do you fight a lot?

JORDAN: Mmm, so so.

HOLLY: What about.

JORDAN: Things.

HOLLY: What was the last thing you fought about?

JORDAN: My driving.

HOLLY: Oh really?

JORDAN: I cut somebody off. It was … nothing too big.

HOLLY: She's very controlling?

JORDAN: She's a very strong woman. It's one of the things about her that I fell in love with and it can also be … frustrating at times.

HOLLY: You get what you pay for.

JORDAN: I suppose.

HOLLY: You from the Islands?

JORDAN: Lord no.

HOLLY: Where are you from?

JORDAN: Tucson Arizona.

HOLLY: You're joking.

JORDAN: No I'm not joking.

HOLLY: You're an American?

JORDAN: My mother and father dragged me kicking and screaming into beautiful downtown Hamilton when I was maybe, oh, nine years old. My father was a member of the Black Panther Party, my mother was one of the original organizers of the Weather Underground. They settled in this here part of the world as a protest of America's oppressive, capitalistic involvement in the suppression of the people's revolution in Vietnam. My father, he had an afro the size of … the size of this table.

HOLLY: Stop.

JORDAN: Not a word of a lie. I used to hide things in it. Pencils, crayons, toy cars. You know those blue and red balls with the white stripe down the middle? I lost one of those for three days.

HOLLY: Oh please.

JORDAN: Only reason why we found it 'cause Dad tripped on the step, fell over, and bounced right back up again.

HOLLY: Stop it.

JORDAN: If I'm lyin' I'm dyin'.

HOLLY: So how'd you two meet?

JORDAN: I beg your pardon?

(HOLLY takes her cigarette back.)

HOLLY: You and your wife. How'd you meet?

JORDAN: Why?

HOLLY: Because I would like to know.

JORDAN: Trans Canada Railroad.

(Music. Lights up on SYLVIA.)

HOLLY: Really.

SYLVIA: He was returning from the University of British Columbia.

JORDAN: Where I had been studying a whack of brand new languages with funky-assed names like ASCII, FORTRAN, and COBAL.

SYLVIA: I was moving from Calgary to the big city.

JORDAN: To become a singer. Soul, reggae, rhythm and blues, jazz. You name it.

SYLVIA: I was across the aisle from him.

JORDAN: And she looked over at me, and asked something like …

SYLVIA: What the hell is that you're reading?

JORDAN: I said something witty like …

SYLVIA: The future.

JORDAN: And she asked me if I could see her future in my book and the next thing you know we're both being very witty and exchanging numbers and promising to keep in touch. She invited me to a concert she was performing at, and I was very, very impressed.

(Music. SYLVIA sings.)

SYLVIA:

I can't sleep at night
I can't eat a bite
'Cause my old man
Don't treat me right.

HOLLY: She's a musician?

JORDAN: Singer. She was a singer.

SYLVIA: Covers. Mostly covers. R 'n' B, blues.

JORDAN: Great voice.

SYLVIA: I played The Silver Dollar, El Mocambo, The Senator.

JORDAN: She had an amazing voice.

SYLVIA: The acoustics at the Senator, oh my Lord.

JORDAN: An amazing voice.

SYLVIA: If the piano hits an E major seventh, and you take the high D, I swear, on my soul, you feel as though you are in the presence of a merciful, compassionate god, and that all is right with the world.

HOLLY: She still sing?

JORDAN: No. No she doesn't.

HOLLY: Why not?

JORDAN: Oh, lots of reasons. Lots of reasons.

HOLLY: That's too bad.

JORDAN: Yeah well.

HOLLY: So you dated, you got married.

(Slides of photos of JORDAN and SYLVIA's hands appear on the painting.)

JORDAN: We dated for a while.

SYLVIA: He had these hands, these big firm hands.

JORDAN: We got married. Had a child.

SYLVIA: He used to make me laugh. He used to make me laugh so hard.

JORDAN: And lived happily ever after.

(The slides fade.)

HOLLY: That's it that's all?

JORDAN: That's it that's all.

HOLLY: Now there, you see? That wasn't so bad now, was it?

JORDAN: Yes it was.

HOLLY: Oh you poor baby.

JORDAN: Are you finished?

HOLLY: Yes I'm done.

JORDAN: Good.

HOLLY: You know, you don't have to try to be a mystery. You are one. You don't have to try.

JORDAN: Yes ma'am.

HOLLY: All right?

JORDAN: Yes ma'am.

HOLLY: Now. I guess we should order a couple of Pakouras and some naan. The Aloo Gobi is excellent here, I …

JORDAN: Holly. I really … I would like to kiss you. Right now. I know we've both been trying very, very hard to dance around it, and I think we've done a pretty good job. But I don't think I will be able to sit here, for the next forty-five minutes, across from you, looking at the shape of your lips, and the way that you move them, and not want to kiss you.

HOLLY: All right.

JORDAN: Just thought you should know.

(HOLLY moves awkwardly closer to him. Their heads slowly move together. SYLVIA's phone rings. They hover over each other's lips. The phone rings again.)

HOLLY: You going to get that? Your phone's ringing, are you going to get that? *Sylvia!!*

(Lights up on SYLVIA and CINDY, her laundry now all folded. HOLLY and JORDAN exit.)

SYLVIA: What?

CINDY: Your phone. You gonna get it or …?

SYLVIA: Hello. I can't talk right now.

(CINDY goes upstairs, taking her laundry with her.)

Then give me Wendle's phone number and I'll call him.

(HOLLY walks down the stairs dressed to kill. She goes to her computer.)

Okay. Yes. Hold on.

(She looks for a pen, HOLLY gives her one.)

Seven five six nine? Got it. Okay. Bye.

(SYLVIA hangs up.)

You're leaving?

HOLLY: In a bit. Okay, let that do its thing. I'm all packed, what am I forgetting. What am I … coffee! Did you want a coffee? I can't remember.

SYLVIA: Uh yes. Yes.

(HOLLY runs off to the kitchen.)

HOLLY: *(Off.)* Cream and sugar?

SYLVIA: Uh, sure. Yes.

HOLLY: *(Off.)* Coming right up.

SYLVIA: So this must be very exciting for you.

HOLLY: *(Off.)* Yeah well sorta. Montreal's my home town so it's, oww! It's not like flying off to Paris or anything, but ...

SYLVIA: And uh, uh ... you uh ...

HOLLY: *(Off.)* What was that?

SYLVIA: Have you uh ...

HOLLY: Have I ...

SYLVIA: So have you two ... uh, you know ... have you uh ...

(HOLLY enters with coffee.)

HOLLY: Done the doo? Not yet. But I am wearing my lucky bra.

(She hands SYLVIA the coffee and heads straight to the computer.)

There were a couple of times when I almost got him to rent a hotel room but ...

SYLVIA: But what?

HOLLY: Well we'd get to the door and he'd start thinking about his wife and kid and ...

SYLVIA: But you didn't give a damn did you.

HOLLY: I beg your pardon.

SYLVIA: That didn't bother you. That didn't stop you. Did it.

(HOLLY goes to work.)

I'm not judging you, I'm not, I'm just curious. I didn't mean to sound judgmental. I didn't. Please go on.

HOLLY: I actually have to focus on this right now.

SYLVIA: No really, I ... Holly? So. So is he ... is he ... is ... is he a ... a good lover?

HOLLY: How do you mean?

SYLVIA: Is he very ... is he passionate.

HOLLY: He can be. After a little coaxing.

(HOLLY steps away from the computer looking for a disk as she speaks. SYLVIA slowly walks up behind her.)

He's patient. That's a change for me and I like it. I have no idea what he's going to be like in bed, but it's a good sign if you know what I mean. And I know you can't always really tell, but when we're ... into it, and he presses up against me, I can feel, that he has got a very nice ...

(SYLVIA tosses her coffee at HOLLY. HOLLY leaps in pain.)

Ahhhh!! *What the—!!*

SYLVIA: I'm sorry.

HOLLY: *What the hell is your problem?!*

SYLVIA: My hand slipped. I'm so sorry.

HOLLY: Don't touch me! Don't ... touch me!!

SYLVIA: Okay. I'm sorry.

(CINDY enters.)

CINDY: What's going on?

SYLVIA: Let me get a towel.

HOLLY: No. It's okay. Just, I need to get cleaned up.

CINDY: You all right?

HOLLY: It's okay, I'm okay. Could you come with me for a second please.

(HOLLY leaves; CINDY follows. SYLVIA sits on the couch. She picks up her cell phone, speed dials.)

SYLVIA: Hey. It's me. I can't talk about it right now. I need you to listen to me very carefully. There was an orange disk on top of the black filing cabinet that had a virus on it. Orange disk. Yes. Do you see it? Yes. Okay. Good. Is there any way that you could get that disk to Bathurst and Bloor in the next five minutes or sooner. I can't. I'll tell you later. No, I need it now. I don't think so but ... uh, *yes,* yes there is another computer that's here that can get e-mail from ... yes. You can do that? How do I ... okay. Okay. Yes I do, hold on. Okay, got a pen? sjones@hotmail.com. So what do I ... okay. How long will it take? Oh really. Fantastic. Okay. And if ...

(CINDY enters with juice.)

SYLVIA: ... you need anything else just give mummy a call, okay, I have to go. Bye.

CINDY: So what happend?

SYLVIA: I was uhm, my, I was turning to look at what she was working on and my foot slipped on ... I am so sorry about ... is she okay?

CINDY: Yeah yeah.

SYLVIA: Do you have the Internet here?

CINDY: Yes we do.

SYLVIA: I just have to get some e-mail.

CINDY: Uh, uhm. Well, okay.

(CINDY goes to the computer. The keyboard has coffee on it.)

CINDY: Eww.

SYLVIA: Sorry about that.

CINDY: S'okay.

SYLVIA: I'll get a rag.

(SYLVIA goes to the kitchen, grabs a rag.)

CINDY: Are you using your own ISP or Hotmail?

SYLVIA: Hotmail. I can uh, I know how to set it up.

CINDY: Okay. Here you go.

(CINDY goes back to the dark room. SYLVIA goes to work. After a moment, HOLLY returns.)

SYLVIA: Again, I am so sorry.

HOLLY: Please, could you not touch my computer please.

(SYLVIA backs away from the computer. HOLLY sits on the couch drying her hair. SYLVIA looks at the computer. All she has to do is press "enter." Her phone rings. She is torn between the computer and her phone. She chooses her phone.)

SYLVIA: Hello? Hey. You just get home? How was school. Oh really.

(HOLLY gets up and starts walking towards her computer.)

Good for you. Yes.

(HOLLY has some water stuck in her ear. She turns down stage and tries to shake it out. SYLVIA creeps towards the computer and presses three keys, and then she briskly walks away from the computer)

It's the green container. It should be on the second shelf next to the ginger ale. Can you see it? Move the hot dog buns. See it now? Okay.

(HOLLY stands and rubs her hair vigorously with the towel as she walks towards the computer.)

I'm going to be away for a while now. Yes. Have you talked to Daddy? What did he say. Really.

(CINDY enters with some prints she just made. She looks at them with a magnifier.)

I can't tell you right now honey, but we'll talk about it all very soon, all right? I promise. Things between your father and I are not good. No. We'll talk about it later, okay? No you may not. No you may not and if I see a charge on my Mastercard at the end of the month then I will take away car privileges for a year. I will. I don't care. Bye.

CINDY: That your daughter?

SYLVIA: Yes.

CINDY: Into getting a movie?

SYLVIA: Certainly.

(HOLLY spanks her computer.)

CINDY: I haven't seen *Rushmore* yet. Have you?

SYLVIA: No. No I haven't. What kind of a movie is it?

CINDY: I don't know. It's supposed to be funny.

(HOLLY spanks her computer.)

SYLVIA: Okay.

CINDY: The place downstairs makes a wicked Roti. We could grab a couple, watch the flick, whaddaya say?

HOLLY: What the hell?

SYLVIA: I uh …

HOLLY: Aw come off it!!

CINDY: What's the matter?

HOLLY: I've got a virus?

CINDY: What?

(CINDY rushes towards her.)

HOLLY: Aw come off it!

CINDY: How did that happen?

HOLLY: I don't know.

CINDY: Don't you have a virus protection program on there?

HOLLY: I hadn't put it on yet.

CINDY: You didn't put it on?

HOLLY: I was going to get around to it, I just …

CINDY: How bad is it?

HOLLY: Everything's … everything's … oh my *God.*

CINDY: Now let's just calm down here, don't panic.

HOLLY: All the *work I did for the past three months, oh my God.*

(SYLVIA goes to the kitchen.)

CINDY: Did you save it on disk. Holly.

HOLLY: Oh God I hate my life.

CINDY: Is there any way you could—

HOLLY: Cindy, I swear to God, it's days like this, I just wish I was dead. I really do.

CINDY: Now just calm down and think. What do you have backed up?

HOLLY: I don't know. Parts of it.

CINDY: How much.

HOLLY: I know she had something to do with it!

CINDY: Holly …

HOLLY: I cannot live here in this apartment with that woman. I told you I didn't want her moving in here and there's no way you're moving out of here and leaving me with her.

CINDY: Is there any way you could use my computer in my room? Holly, is there any way …

HOLLY: It's a different …

CINDY: Can you rent one, can you …

(HOLLY stands.)

HOLLY: But …

CINDY: You name it. What.

HOLLY: But if I loaded stuff onto your hard drive …

CINDY: Do it.

HOLLY: What do you have on your computer …

CINDY: Some letters to my dad. Some stuff for the wedding. Nothing important.

HOLLY: I might have to erase all that.

CINDY: Holly, do it. Go. Do what you need to do.

(HOLLY kisses CINDY on the cheek.)

HOLLY: I owe you so much. I know I do. And I'm gonna pay you back for everything, I swear to God. I am. Really.

CINDY: Do what you have to do, okay? Go.

(HOLLY runs upstairs. SYLVIA enters.)

You hungry?

SYLVIA: Yes I am.

(CINDY hands her a flyer from the restaurant downstairs. SYLVIA goes for her purse.)

CINDY: Pick your Roti: shrimp, goat, chicken, vegetarian.

SYLVIA: Chicken.

(SYLVIA gives her money.)

CINDY: This is too much.

SYLVIA: It's for everyone. Dinner's on me.

CINDY: I couldn't let you do that.

SYLVIA: I insist.

CINDY: But …

SYLVIA: I insist.

CINDY: If … you insist.

SYLVIA: I do.

CINDY: Chicken?

SYLVIA: Yes.

(CINDY leaves. Music. "Solitude" by Billy Holiday. SYLVIA packs up her computer and files and takes everything upstairs.

End of Act One.)

Act Two

(At rise the stage is empty. Music.

CINDY creeps out of the kitchen with a broom. SYLVIA creeps down the stairs with a shovel.)

SYLVIA: *(Voiceover.)* There was a time when, if you were to ask me about the early blues, the classic blues, I would have spouted out names like Ma Rainey and Bessie Smith. I would have given you opinions culled from bar room conversations, mingled with my own first impressions.

CINDY: I think it's under the couch.

SYLVIA: *(Voiceover.)* Then one day, I just happened to walk into a record shop on Queen Street. They were playing Victoria Spivey's "Any-Kind-A-Man" and over the next two hours I was lost in a whole world of classic blues singers whose names don't easily come to mind.

(They knock at the couch. Nothing. They creep around, all over the apartment, looking.)

SYLVIA: Think it might have crept back into—

CINDY: Shhh.

SYLVIA: *(Voiceover.)* Sippie Wallace, Ida Cox, Alberta Hunter, Mary Johnson, Margaret Johnson, Mamie Smith and more. Many more. These women tore open their souls, cannibalized the pain in their lives. And none of them would live long enough to see the way in which their work transformed popular culture well into the twenty-first century.

CINDY: Hear that?

SYLVIA: *(Voiceover.)* It's a real shame we do not control when we enter this world or when we leave it.

(The rat runs between CINDY's legs.)

CINDY: Ah!

(SYLVIA chases the rat to a corner and smashes it with her shovel. Blood splurts on the wall, and on some of HOLLY's artwork.)

I didn't need to see that.

SYLVIA: Do you have a dustpan, or a …

CINDY: Kitchen.

(SYLVIA goes to the kitchen to get a paper towel. HOLLY enters with food.)

I didn't need to …

(CINDY looks at the dead rat.)

Aww.

HOLLY: What.

CINDY: Don't look. We just killed a rat.

(HOLLY looks.)

HOLLY: You ordered the goat right?

(HOLLY hands her the Roti. SYLVIA returns with a dustpan, paper towels, and a garbage can.)

SYLVIA: I think there may be some blood on your artwork there.

HOLLY: Oh yeah.

SYLVIA: I have some paper towels here if you …

HOLLY: I just might want to leave it there, hold on.

(HOLLY looks at her work. SYLVIA scoops up the rat and puts it in the garbage.)

CINDY: I really shouldn't have looked at that.

HOLLY: Oh stop being such a baby.

CINDY: I can't take blood, I really can't.

SYLVIA: After your first child, you get over it.

HOLLY: Great.

SYLVIA: What you do not get over is not being able to sit on a toilet for a month.

HOLLY: Please.

SYLVIA: Having to use a spray bottle to clean your behind because …

HOLLY: I am about to eat please. Thank you.

CINDY: I opened a red.

HOLLY: Which one.

CINDY: Inniskilin Marocheal Foch.

HOLLY: What year.

CINDY: Ninety-seven.

HOLLY: Fine.

CINDY: Want a glass?

SYLVIA: No thank you.

CINDY: Wine won't interfere with the cranberry thing will it?

SYLVIA: I don't know.

(CINDY thinks about it, then goes to the kitchen. HOLLY notices SYLVIA is staring at her.)

HOLLY: Can I help you?

(Pause.)

SYLVIA: So this man that you're seeing …

HOLLY: Yes.

SYLVIA: Did he ever tell you anything about … some of the things that are going wrong in his relationship with his wife?

HOLLY: Why?

SYLVIA: I … I'm … I'm fa—… I'm curious. *(She was going to say she was fascinated.)*

HOLLY: Why?

SYLVIA: Why?

HOLLY: Yeah, why.

CINDY: *(Off.)* When were you planning on doing these dishes?

HOLLY: I'll get to them.

(HOLLY looks around.)

SYLVIA: Relationships …

CINDY: *(Off.)* They've been here for three days.

HOLLY: I've been busy.

(CINDY enters with two plastic cups.)

SYLVIA: I know that you really appreciate people being honest, and I guess the situation fascinates me because I … something inside of me tells me that I could … learn something from you. I guess.

HOLLY: I highly doubt that anything I say could possibly help you in your life Sylvia.

CINDY: What are we talking about?

HOLLY: She wants to know what's going wrong in Jordan's marriage.

CINDY: And?

HOLLY: And what?

CINDY: What'd you tell her?

HOLLY: I didn't tell her anything. It's none of her business.

CINDY: Do you know?

HOLLY: What?

CINDY: Have you ever asked him why he's cheating on his wife?

HOLLY: No.

CINDY: You never asked him?

HOLLY: But, I mean, why would I ask him that, I mean, it's none of my business.

CINDY: You know, sometimes you absolutely mystify me.

HOLLY: Oh come on!

CINDY: Completely mystify me.

HOLLY: What's to know?! They don't click any more, he wants something else. What?!

CINDY: Is this a relationship you're having with him or what?

HOLLY: I don't know.

CINDY: Do you want it to be a relationship?

HOLLY: I haven't decided yet.

CINDY: I am going to say this to you one more time, and I really want you to listen to me so that you hear the words that I'm saying to you. You cannot have a relationship with a man who wants to stay married to his wife. You can't do it. It doesn't work.

HOLLY: Don't condescend to me.

CINDY: I'm not condescending to you, I just think that sometimes you don't think about the consequences of your actions.

HOLLY: It's a thing. It's just a little thing. It's not a big deal. What do you care? He's not your husband.

CINDY: That's not the point.

HOLLY: Marriage doesn't mean anything. You said it yourself.

CINDY: I never said—

HOLLY: You said, about what's-her-face—

CINDY: Holly, her name is Arlene, not what's-her-face.

HOLLY: You said that your marriage to Arlene is nothing but a hollow mimicry of an antiquated patriarchal ritual. You said that.

CINDY: I said—

HOLLY: You said the only reason why you were going through with this is because you feel it is an important political statement, but—

CINDY: Bah bah bup bup, can I speak for a second now, please. All right. For the tenth time, I said that marriage doesn't prove that you love someone. That's what I said. Both Arlene and I believe that it is a legal status that should be available to everyone and anyone who want it, but no it is not proof that love exists between two people. No.

HOLLY: Then why get married.

CINDY: Because I want to get married.

HOLLY: Why? It doesn't mean you love each other. Personally, I think we need a whole new way of looking at modern relationships. I do. I think … don't do your little smirk thing, that really irritates me. I think there should be three stages; the person with whom you have a youthful, passionate, self-destructive relationship. Then you have a mature relationship, the person you have children with, buy a house with, create a home with, et cetera. And then, you have the next stage. Whatever that is. Someone to grow old with, the person who is closer to who you've become. Whatever. I think we should just accept that's the way we are, it's human nature. It's the way your parents were, that's the way my parents were, let's just admit it instead of creating this culture of guilt around broken marriages, and making people feel like they've failed at something that is simply not in our genetic make-up. "Hey, we had some good times together, we raised children, that's important enough, things didn't work out. You go your way, I'll go mine. Let's move on."

SYLVIA: Life must be very easy for you.

HOLLY: I beg your pardon?

SYLVIA: Things don't work out, you just throw it away. You can say you love someone but you don't have to mean it because hey, people change their minds. It's human. They grow, they become different. Tell me something. Do you value anything in life? Is there anything you hold sacred, anything you would make a sacrifice for? Or is everything about you? Everything simply put on this earth to fulfill your pleasures, and nothing else. Let me tell you something, life is short, very short. Shorter than you think right now. You can live for yourself, for the … the pleasure of the moment, or you can grow up, stop behaving like a child, become responsible for your actions and give something to life instead of constantly taking things away.

CINDY: I have some prints to finish.

(CINDY leaves. HOLLY grabs her cigarettes.)

HOLLY: I really don't think it's a good idea that you live here.

(HOLLY follows CINDY to the darkroom. SYLVIA takes out her pill bottles. JORDAN enters.)

JORDAN: What I said to the marriage counsellor was if I am going to come back into the house: (a) the dynamics of the relationship had to change. At that point in time Maja was eight—

SYLVIA: She was nine.

JORDAN: She was …

(He decides not to start an argument.)

I could see, it was blatant to me that they were … there was a conflict in their relationship. Maja was demanding more independence at an earlier age than—

SYLVIA: She was a royal pain in the …

JORDAN: The way you were—

SYLVIA: … ass! And you defended her because—

JORDAN: The way you were responding to her was not proportionate to—

SYLVIA: You were never there!

JORDAN: I know.

SYLVIA: You were never there! You were off—

JORDAN: Can I finish—

SYLVIA: Late night at the office, business trip to Calgary, to Hamilton—

JORDAN: It's the sanctimonious tone that—

SYLVIA: While I have to make dinner, I have to clean, I can't get you to take out the damn garbage without a ten-minute explanation of …

JORDAN: May I continue?

SYLVIA: … how you work so hard, how you provide for—

JORDAN: (a) the dynamics of our relationship—

SYLVIA: Why don't you talk about some of the things you said to me.

JORDAN: I—

SYLVIA: Why don't you talk about some of the things you said to me. I know you like to be seen as the … why don't you talk about some of the hurtful things you've said to me? Why don't you.

JORDAN: Okay, look, some of the … I admit that … I have said some terrible, terrible things to you. Yes.

SYLVIA: Remember what you said to me on Maja's ninth birthday?

JORDAN: I made a comment once, it was in the middle of an argument, I said something derogatory, to the effect of how her body had changed since we had first met.

SYLVIA: What did you say to me once we had come back from the hospital? What did you say to me. Look at me. Three days before our eleventh wedding anniversary what did you say to me?

JORDAN: It was in response to something you said to me.

SYLVIA: What did I say to you.

JORDAN: You know what …

SYLVIA: What did I say to you.

JORDAN: … you said to me.

SYLVIA: What did I say to you.

JORDAN: I can't repeat it.

SYLVIA: Why?

JORDAN: *You know why I can't!!* You know why. You know why I can't … Jesus. Jesus Lord, God. Please. Please.

SYLVIA: The dynamics of the relationship had to change.

(JORDAN pulls out a handkerchief and dabs the corners of his eyes.)

JORDAN: It was suggested that holding on to … to every little slight was not going to provide solutions for the future.

SYLVIA: We agreed.

JORDAN: I promised that I would move from programming to the marketing department. It would mean a cut in pay, but I would have more time for … my family.

SYLVIA: And I promised that I would seek counselling. That what was happening to me, what was happening to my body … I admitted that I had been focusing a lot of the rage I was feeling about my situation on others. And with help, I could work on that.

JORDAN: One thing you must know … two, two things you must know.

SYLVIA: I'm going to be fine.

(CINDY enters trying to open an immersion tank.)

JORDAN: I will always be there for you. I will always be there for you.

CINDY: Is the dishrag still out here?

SYLVIA: I don't know.

(CINDY bangs it on a table.)

CINDY: I just need to ...

SYLVIA: Here.

(SYLVIA takes the container and tries to open it.)

CINDY: I'm sorry about that.

SYLVIA: About?

CINDY: The whole ... thing here.

SYLVIA: Oh, don't ...

CINDY: No, I uh ... I've ... I'm used to her ... rants. I'm sure, from the outside it must seem ...

SYLVIA: Perhaps I crossed a line. I apologize.

CINDY: I ... I think ... I don't think you feel very comfortable here. And you can correct me if I'm wrong, but I kind of get the sense that you're going through some pretty heavy stuff in your life right now and ... but ... uhm, I don't know how best to say this ... I don't think this is going to work out.

SYLVIA: All right.

CINDY: We are going to do our best to get your money back to you.

SYLVIA: All right.

CINDY: It may take some time, but ...

(HOLLY storms out of the darkroom.)

HOLLY: I would like you out please.

CINDY: Holly, I am handling it.

HOLLY: And could you not drink my wine any more please.

(CINDY grabs her wallet.)

I think it would be best if, you, like, want wine, you should just get your own. Okay? Thank you.

CINDY: Here.

HOLLY: I don't want your money.

CINDY: Here's twenty bucks.

HOLLY: *(Simultaneously with CINDY's next line.)* I don't want your money, okay? It's not about the money, it's about respecting me and respecting my wishes. Cindy. I don't want it.

CINDY: *(Simultaneously with HOLLY.)* This should get you a replacement for what I drank. Okay? It's all right. I've got a job. I can get more of this. When I do work, you know what? It's funny, when I do work, they give me this stuff. It's called money? It helps to pay for things like groceries and rent and stuff. It's great, you should try it.

(HOLLY walks back upstairs. SYLVIA opens the container.)

SYLVIA: Here.

CINDY: I would like you to answer a question for me.

(CINDY runs to a cabinet and pulls out her wedding dress. She holds it to her body.)

Okay. What do you think this material is.

(SYLVIA touches the dress. Memories of SYLVIA's own wedding flood back to her.)

SYLVIA: Feels like silk.

CINDY: I wasn't sure if it was silk or a cotton blend kinda thing.

SYLVIA: I think it's silk.

(CINDY gives it to SYLVIA. SYLVIA holds it up with her good arm.)

CINDY: I got it at this store in Kensington market. Two hundred forty bucks. With tax, two hundred seventy. Around two hundred seventy.

SYLVIA: It's ... beautiful.

CINDY: Well, you know, I mean, I thought at the time, hey, get it now, or else who knows, right? And I just, when I saw it, I just knew that this had to be it. It's just simple. You know? And it fits perfectly.

SYLVIA: It's beautiful.

CINDY: And you can laugh all you want. My mother laughed at me, my sister ... I don't care. I'm gonna get a weave. I'm gonna do it. I figure the one day of my life I would ever wear a weave in my hair, it would be my wedding day.

SYLVIA: I'll tell you something. There's a place just up the street from here on Bathurst.

(SYLVIA pulls out her wallet.)

CINDY: Okay.

SYLVIA: I can't remember the name. But it's just up the street, you can't miss it. That's where I take my daughter.

(SYLVIA pulls a picture of her daughter out of her wallet.)

CINDY: This her?

SYLVIA: This is my daughter.

CINDY: She's a heartbreaker.

SYLVIA: That's from a couple of years ago.

CINDY: What's her name?

SYLVIA: Maja.

CINDY: I love that name.

SYLVIA: She's just finishing her last year of high school.

CINDY: You want to hear my mom's joke about having a daughter?

SYLVIA: Okay.

CINDY: "Me neva wan have no daughta. With a son, ya haffa worry 'bout one penis. With a daughta, you haffa worry about all the penises all ova the whole *world*."

(SYLVIA laughs.)

SYLVIA: Your mother is a very wise woman.

CINDY: She seemed to think so.

SYLVIA: Very wise woman.

CINDY: Wanna see my lover?

SYLVIA: All right.

(CINDY pulls out a photo from her wallet.)

CINDY: That's her on the left.

SYLVIA: It's a ... she seems like a very nice person.

CINDY: Look at that chin.

SYLVIA: That's a very nice chin.

(CINDY gets herself a glass of wine.)

CINDY: We met actually while I was temping at Wood Gundy. She's a sales representative for a company that makes water purifiers. She came in and just kinda ... swept me off my feet.

SYLVIA: I see.

CINDY: Wine?

SYLVIA: No, thank you.

CINDY: Originally we were going to flip to see who wore the dress and who'd wear the tux, but ever since she asked me to marry her, it's like I've just lost my mind. I'm picking out floral patterns, designing the invites, and I love it. I love the ritual, the stupid quirky traditions. I'm just totally loving being a girl. I love it.

SYLVIA: Really.

CINDY: We did the whole shower thing, I met her mom. Her parents are totally cool. She got to meet my mum and my sister. My dad ... he's not ... it's not important to me that she meet my dad.

SYLVIA: I see.

CINDY: He is someone ... as I get closer to the wedding, I'm trying to simplify my life, you know? Surround myself with people who provide a positive energy. For my mental health, my physical health, I think that's really important to do.

SYLVIA: It is important.

CINDY: I think sometimes we underestimate exactly how important it is, the role positive energy plays in keeping yourself healthy, you know?

SYLVIA: Yes it is very important. To keep positive, stay positive and optimistic, and keep positive things around you, positive outlook on life. Yes it is important. People keep saying that to me, so it must be true. Right? And I keep feeling ... it's almost like someone is telling you to jump off a cliff and if you just believe, if you just stay positive and believe, then you're gonna fly. Everything in your life, all your life, has told you that if you jump off a cliff, you will fall to the ground to your death, but you have this special person beside you, telling you things that make you believe. And he's not perfect, but then neither am I. And one day you find out he's been unfaithful to you. That he's lied to you. And you don't know what to do. You really don't. You can't say what you want to say because ... because if you do, then you risk losing him. Forever. And you can't do that. Not now. Not right now. No. You can't. Cannot. No matter what he's done, you're gonna have to work through it. Work through everything. We've worked through bigger than this, we're just gonna have to work through it, because ... because there's no way, there is not a snowball's chance in hell, that I am going to be able to jump off that cliff all by myself. There is no way. Not alone. There's no way.

(CINDY grabs a Kleenex. She hands it to SYLVIA.)

CINDY: Sylvia, I really would like you to tell me what's going on.

(SYLVIA dabs her eyes with the Kleenex.)

SYLVIA: You wanna know what's going on.

CINDY: I would. Yes.

SYLVIA: All right. All right. But, you have to promise me that you won't say anything to Holly about what I'm about to tell you, all right? I mean it. It will just be between you and me. All right? You promise me?

CINDY: I promise.

SYLVIA: I mean it now. Can I trust you to keep a secret?

CINDY: Oh trust me, I … she won't hear anything from me. Really.

SYLVIA: All right. All right. Now …

(There is knock at the door.)

CINDY: Hold on a second.

(Another knock.)

Coming. Coming.

(She goes to the door.)

JORDAN: *(Off.)* Is Holly there?

CINDY: Oh great. Holly!

(CINDY goes down the steps to the front door. SYLVIA panics, and looks for a place to hide. There is more knocking.)

CINDY: *(Off.)* Yeah she's here. Just hold your horses.

JORDAN: *(Off.)* Hey Cindy.

CINDY: *(Off.)* It's Cynthia.

JORDAN: *(Off.)* Right.

CINDY: *(Off.)* Can I help you?

(SYLVIA finds a place to hide amongst Holly's art.)

JORDAN: *(Off.)* Can I come in?

CINDY: *(Off.)* Sure.

(CINDY enters with JORDAN.)

JORDAN: Thanks.

CINDY: No pro—

JORDAN: What's the matter?

(CINDY looks for SYLVIA.)

CINDY: Uh, nothing. Don't worry about it. Holly, you've got a visitor.

(HOLLY enters.)

HOLLY: I heard you the first time.

CINDY: Whatever.

(CINDY goes to her darkroom.)

HOLLY: Hey honey.

JORDAN: You ready?

HOLLY: Oh my God.

JORDAN: What?

HOLLY: I didn't call you.

JORDAN: What's the matter.

HOLLY: I can't go.

JORDAN: What?

HOLLY: I forgot to call you.

JORDAN: What's wrong?

HOLLY: I've got a virus.

JORDAN: I beg your pardon?

HOLLY: On the computer. A computer virus.

JORDAN: Right. Okay.

HOLLY: I have to install a bunch of stuff on Cindy's machine, re-do everything from scratch …

JORDAN: We're not going to Montreal, are we.

HOLLY: I'm so sorry honey.

JORDAN: No. You … this is more important.

HOLLY: Can I make it up to you?

JORDAN: No, it's okay.

HOLLY: Let me give you a quickie.

JORDAN: I don't want our first time to be a quickie.

HOLLY: You're such a romantic.

(They move towards each other to kiss. They get a static electricity shock.)

Oww.

JORDAN: You need a humidifier in this place.

(She tries to take off his pants.)

HOLLY: We've got a humidifier.

JORDAN: Then why don't you use it?

HOLLY: It needs fixin'. You gonna fix it for me mister man?

JORDAN: Holly.

HOLLY: Come.

JORDAN: Have you eaten?

HOLLY: Yes I have.

JORDAN: I've got the bags in the car, I got the tickets …

HOLLY: Is there any way you could get a refund? How about change it to next weekend?

JORDAN: I don't know.

HOLLY: Oh, you poor thing.

(She goes to kiss him. He touches her hand. They kiss. She starts to take his clothes off.)

JORDAN: Come to Montreal with me.

HOLLY: Look, if I don't hand this in by Monday morning at nine o'clock, they will give the job to somebody else, they give the job to somebody else, I can't pay the rent, I can't pay Cindy back, I can't pay you back …

JORDAN: I won't bring it up again. I won't. Go back to work. Go.

(She does.)

HOLLY: I thought, we had a deal about the, the L-word.

JORDAN: Yes we did.

HOLLY: What happened.

JORDAN: I broke that deal didn't I.

HOLLY: Yes you did.

JORDAN: I didn't mean to it just kinda came out.

HOLLY: Yeah, well, that's fine but like, you're not, this isn't changing into something else is it?

JORDAN: What do you think.

HOLLY: It can't.

JORDAN: Then it won't.

HOLLY: I'm serious.

JORDAN: So am I.

HOLLY: Wait, just stop. Look at me. Look at me. Do you love me? Do you?

JORDAN: No. No I don't. No.

HOLLY: Okay.

JORDAN: There are things I love about you, but I do not love you, *per se.*

HOLLY: Jordan …

JORDAN: That's allowed isn't it? I love being in your presence. I don't love you. There's a difference.

HOLLY: You are such an ass.

(They kiss.)

JORDAN: I seem to recall you saying you loved me back.

HOLLY: Well what the hell was I supposed to say?

JORDAN: "Now Jordan, what did we say about the L-word." "You know how I feel about the L-word." You could have said any one of a number of things. You're so direct, up-front, honest, that's one of the things I love about you. Sorry.

(They kiss.)

HOLLY: Sometimes I think that certain desires bind us to a particular fate.

JORDAN: Think so?

HOLLY: To desire a thing and you are immediately tied forever to its fate.

JORDAN: I love you.

HOLLY: I know you do.

(They kiss. Long, passionate. She feels herself slipping deeper and deeper. She pulls his face away. Holds it in her hands.)

Why are you doing this?

JORDAN: What?

HOLLY: You've told me all about how you feel so guilty, and about how you really respect your wife and your daughter, and you don't want to hurt them, but why are you doing this?

JORDAN: How do you mean?

HOLLY: The sex with your wife is awful, right?

JORDAN: Holly.

HOLLY: She doesn't understand you any more, right?

JORDAN: Sure. Okay.

HOLLY: What happened.

JORDAN: A lot of things happened.

HOLLY: And suddenly you had to stop hiding and pretending and deal with how you truly felt about each other.

JORDAN: I thought we had an understanding that I wouldn't go into all this.

HOLLY: I love you too baby.

JORDAN: Very good. Very good.

HOLLY: Why don't you tell her? About us. Why don't you tell her?

JORDAN: Do you have children?

HOLLY: You know I don't.

JORDAN: Then back off a little.

HOLLY: No you back off a little. What do you think this is? You can just come in here, jump around and say I love you and think that it's not going to affect me in some way?

(She holds his face.)

I just finished putting my heart away in a tiny little box with a big huge lock on it and hid it away in a deep dark hole in my psyche. If I'm going to even think about opening up that door again you better believe I'm going to be extra careful about who I open it for. You understand? Do you understand me?

JORDAN: Yes I do.

HOLLY: Okay. Now. What are you going to tell your wife?

JORDAN: I don't know.

HOLLY: Give it a shot.

JORDAN: I don't want to.

(She puts his arms around her.)

HOLLY: Darling wife, I called you here this evening because I want to tell you that I have found myself a nubile twenty-something who actually likes having sex with me and who makes me feel like I'm not a forty-one-year-old who is incapable of facing the fact that maybe I am a failure at being a husband. And instead of dedicating myself to the marriage, I am going to run off to my mistress whom I will screw, and screw often.

(She puts his hands on her breasts.)

And I will make an attempt at some kind of a relationship with this young thing. And one day, I am going to wake up, and look over at her, and I will realize that I was not running away from you dear wife, I was running away from something inside me.

(She steps away from him.)

Something that is still inside me. And I will leave my poor, gullible, young mistress and I will wander this earth until my bones are too weak to hold me up, and I will die knowing myself even less than I ever did at any other point in my life.

(She kisses her finger and touches his lip.)

JORDAN: I guess I should let you get back to work.

HOLLY: I guess I should get back to work.

(JORDAN walks towards the door, and stops.)

JORDAN: Do you know what a telomerase is?

HOLLY: No I do not.

JORDAN: It is the enzyme that allows malignant cells to produce endlessly in a carcinoma. A carcinoma is the kind of growth that attacks epithelial tissue, such as the lining of the body cavities and organs, and the glandular tissue of the prostate and breast.

HOLLY: All right.

JORDAN: Three days before our eleventh wedding anniversary, my wife was diagnosed with a malignant carcinoma of the breast. And it was something ... that I don't think either of us handled very well. We were going through a really bad period at the time. We separated for a bit, we did some counselling and we were persuaded to believe that neither of us wanted to deal with the potential loss of the other. We had gone through so much, we had fought so hard, for so long to stay together, and the idea that one of us could be taken away by something as simple, as rudimentary as mortality, it scared us. And so we came together, and we worked through it, we worked hard. Very, very hard. She had an operation, and I gave her what she wanted, what she needed. I worked hard on trying to be the kind of man my better nature knows I can be. And then one day, she's in the hospital, getting samples taken for testing, I'm doing a trade show, and I meet this young, precocious woman with a fierce, vibrant intelligence, with a hot body, beautiful thighs ...

HOLLY: You like my thighs?

JORDAN: My God, Holly, your thighs make me weep. And I, in a moment of weakness, I feel, for an instant, like I'm another person. I feel like I've been allowed to be someone who I almost thought had completely disappeared forever. I could speak to someone and there was no weight to every utterance. No triple meaning, no decoding decades' worth of minute behavior and motivations. And I return to my wife, and I returned to my role, but that moment of weakness has turned into a kind of burning self-awareness that doesn't let you sleep. It doesn't let you eat. It invades every impulse for every action you perform all day long. I always thought I was the kind of man who would be strong enough to see this sort of thing through, but I'm not. I always thought that I was the kind of man who could just focus on what I knew had to be done, I would get through this. And perhaps I used to be, but now, I can't. I can't. I can't. I ... I can't. I've never done this before. I haven't. So I ask you to forgive me if I am too eager, or if I underestimate the complexity of your position. In two days they will provide my wife with the results of the test they performed to see where and how much the cancer has spread.

Once she receives those results, I will be informing my wife that I intend to leave her. Regardless of what happens between us, that is what I will be telling her. Now I know that this is a lot of new information, but I think we already have a lot of things in common. I think a connection has been made between you and I and ... I would like it to continue. That's all I know. Nothing else. Now I'll let you get back to your work.

HOLLY: All right.

JORDAN: I would like you to give me a call when you finish.

HOLLY: I will.

(JORDAN leaves. HOLLY goes after him to lock the door. SYLVIA enters. The front door closes. HOLLY returns. She sees SYLVIA.)

Where did you come from?

SYLVIA: I don't know.

(HOLLY grabs her cigarettes.)

HOLLY: I, uh, excuse me.

(HOLLY leaves to have a cigarette. CINDY enters with a bundle of photos, drinking from her cranberry juice container. SYLVIA quickly hides her tears.)

CINDY: Hey, you all right?

SYLVIA: I'm fine.

CINDY: You sure?

SYLVIA: Please don't come near me.

CINDY: I have to run out and drop something off, but I'll be back.

SYLVIA: You're leaving.

CINDY: Yeah.

SYLVIA: When will you be back?

CINDY: I'm not sure, could be a couple of minutes, could be longer.

SYLVIA: Okay. Okay.

CINDY: If you want we can talk then.

SYLVIA: Uhm, sure. Fine.

CINDY: See ya in a bit.

(CINDY grabs her bike and her knapsack with the photos and goes.

Music.

SYLVIA goes to the ceremonial knife. She takes it in her hand. HOLLY enters. SYLVIA hides the knife behind her back. HOLLY takes out her bottle of Beaujolais. She opens it, grabs a glass, and pours the wine.)

HOLLY: My skin is so dry.

SYLVIA: Maybe you shouldn't drink so much.

HOLLY: You think it's the alcohol?

(HOLLY downs the entire glass of wine.)

SYLVIA: Could be.

(SYLVIA pulls out the knife. She slowly walks up to HOLLY. HOLLY begins to cry. SYLVIA slowly lowers the knife and drops it behind her, out of sight. She puts her hand on HOLLY's shoulder. HOLLY puts her hand on SYLVIA's. She drops the glass on the couch and turns towards SYLVIA, hugs her.)

HOLLY: I'm so sorry.

SYLVIA: It's all right.

HOLLY: I'm so sorry. I …

SYLVIA: Shhh.

(HOLLY grabs a Kleenex, cleans her face, grabs her cigarettes, and lights one.)

HOLLY: I was thinking about what you said. You're right. I am selfish. I borrow money without any real intention of paying it back. I take from everything around me because I want to hide from myself the fact that I am a failure as an artist, which is all I ever wanted to be. All I can be. I am having an affair with a married man because I crave false intimacy, and when he offers me commitment, I feel nothing but dread. And sometimes, this little voice inside my head, tells me to open up that bottle of Maristol Beaujolais, get real drunk, go down to the Spadina subway station, jump down onto the tracks, where that sharp curve would prevent a conductor from seeing your body, shut your eyes and head on off to something else. Because I can't stay here. I really can't.

SYLVIA: Sometimes you can get so down, you can feel so depressed about your situation, you can't really think straight. You start thinking about doing something foolish. Something you know you shouldn't do.

HOLLY: Yeah.

SYLVIA: I know what that feels like.

HOLLY: Really?

SYLVIA: Then a few moments pass, and you start to … if you give yourself a moment, you start to realize certain things. Certain things start to become clear.

HOLLY: Like what.

SYLVIA: You can be betrayed by your family, your friends, your husband, your children. You can be betrayed by your own body. In a way, the only thing you have left, that is sacred, that is true, is the faith that you put into yourself. It's something you can forget sometimes. It may be something you can think about.

HOLLY: Would you like some wine?

SYLVIA: Yes I think I would.

HOLLY: Stay right here.

(HOLLY goes to the kitchen. SYLVIA takes the knife and puts it back where it came from.)

SYLVIA: Sometimes the humidifier on a furnace can become corroded with lime deposits.

HOLLY: *(Off.)* Oh yeah.

SYLVIA: It's pretty easy to open up. Take a look at it. You may have to replace the filter.

(CINDY enters from the front door. Just as SYLVIA finishes placing the knife back where it came from. HOLLY returns with a glass of wine for SYLVIA.)

CINDY: What's up?

HOLLY: If you want to taste a three-thousand-dollar wine you better go to the kitchen, grab a glass, get some crackers, and grab that raw-milk Brie in the fridge door.

CINDY: All right.

(CINDY goes to the kitchen. HOLLY starts looking for the phone.)

SYLVIA: What are you looking for?

HOLLY: Have you seen the phone around anywhere?

(SYLVIA realizes what she must do. She rushes to her purse, pulls out her phone and hands it to HOLLY.)

SYLVIA: Here.

HOLLY: No I couldn't.

SYLVIA: I insist.

HOLLY: It's okay, I can …

SYLVIA: Please. Please. Use my cell. Really. It's fine. Really.

HOLLY: Okay. Thanks.

SYLVIA: My pleasure.

(HOLLY takes her phone and dials.)

HOLLY: Wanna put some music on?

SYLVIA: Certainly.

(SYLVIA goes to her purse and takes her CD out of her portable CD player.)

HOLLY: It's ringing.

SYLVIA: He may not answer right away.

HOLLY: Oh that's right, he's got call display. He's probably wondering ... Hello?

(Back to phone.)

Hey. I think I need to see you right now. Right now. Bye.

(She hangs up.)

SYLVIA: Is he coming?

HOLLY: He said he'd be here right away.

SYLVIA: Really.

HOLLY: Yes.

(SYLVIA starts to prepare herself.)

SYLVIA: Okay. Okay. Good. That's very good.

HOLLY: You all right?

SYLVIA: Holly, for the first time, in a long time, I can truly say that I'm going to be just fine.

(CINDY enters.)

CINDY: Now what the hell is going on in here?

HOLLY: Just bring your glass over here and shut up. Let me rephrase that. Please, bring your glass over here and shut up.

CINDY: *(Sucking her teeth.)* Lawd have mercy.

HOLLY: Sylvia, what do you think of the wine?

SYLVIA: What do you think?

HOLLY: I think it tastes like stewed urine. *(HOLLY laughs.)* I paid three thousand dollars, for a bottle of Maristol Beaujolais, and it tastes like stewed urine.

SYLVIA: You got the three-thousand-dollar wine blues.

HOLLY: I got the three-thousand-dollar-plus-GST blues.

(They take a sip.)

Where's that music you were going to put on?

CINDY: I got it.

(CINDY takes the CD from SYLVIA. She starts the music.)

HOLLY: Whose CD is this?

SYLVIA: It's mine.

CINDY: This has got to be Lady Day.

SYLVIA: Ha! No, no it's not.

HOLLY: Who is this.

CINDY: No, don't tell me, I want to figure it out.

(CINDY starts to dance with the music.)

SYLVIA: Now I have to say something. In a few moments when he gets here, things are going to start moving pretty rapidly. Things are going to be said that, well, are hurtful. You and I are going to part, and we may never speak to each other again. Let me finish. But I want you to know, I wish we had met in a different time, under different circumstances. I think that would have been nice.

HOLLY: Okay.

(Lights slowly fade. CINDY encourages SYLVIA to dance with her. She does. HOLLY is perplexed by what SYLVIA just said.)

SYLVIA: *(Voiceover.)*
Most people
When they sing
Fling their arms to their sides
And try to leave the ground
But to sing the blues
To sing the blues
You plant yourself into this earth
You claim that which makes you weak
You take your pain as a gift
And this short life
Becomes as wide and full
As breath.

(HOLLY slowly looks at SYLVIA. She drops her glass. She knows.

Blackout.)